This book belongs to:

_____

Phillippeans 4:13 → I can do all things throug Christ
who strengthens ME

On 5/3 I weighed in at 176.6

had a banana + grapes for breckfast

peanuts + veggies

Dinner I had a healthy salad

5/4 I had oatmeal with some granola
and an apple.

Made in the USA
Middletown, DE
19 November 2019

78980076R00066